WHAT DO ANGELS DO?

Helen Glowacki

Novels by Helen Glowacki
When God Broke Grandma's Heart
When God Took Grandma Home
When Grandma Chased the Spirits
The Granddaughter and the Monkey Swing
The Story of God's Plan of Salvation
Abiding Faith, Hidden Treasure
And Then They Asked God
Caleb's Testimony

Why God Why Series by Helen Glowacki
To What Purpose?
Why God Why?
Why Trust Scripture?
Life after Death And The Coming Tribulation
What Does God Want Me To Do RIGHT NOW?
Do Our Little Sins *Really* Count?
What Do Angels Do?

Other non-fiction Books by Helen Glowacki
Politically Incorrect: When Enough is Enough
Overcoming Depression: How to be Happy
What No One Is Telling You about Addictions

****

Authors Website: www.helenglowacki.com

Face book: http://www.facebook.com/pages/The-Grandmother-Series/155300907853909?ref=ts and also http://www.facebook.com/pages/Helenglowacki/

WHAT DO ANGELS DO?

Helen Glowacki

MISSION STATEMENT

To Serve

God

With All Our Strength

And

All Our Heart

Helen Glowacki

NOTE TO THE READER

The King James Version (KJV) of the Bible, which is public domain in the United States, is used throughout all the books written by this author. For further study, the author recommends the New King James Version (NKJV) of the Bible as easier reading and less usage of the old world language while remaining true to the original text.

ACKNOWLEDGEMENTS

Special thanks to my husband Wally who provides so much support to my work and makes my computer behave. Thanks to my children and grandchildren for the constancy of their love and encouragement, and to Reverend Herold Ambroise for his fervent prayers on my behalf. Special thanks to Richard Levinson for providing the first opportunity through which I could develop my writing skills, to my brothers and sisters and ministers in faith who give so freely of their love and prayers, and to my Face book friends who also pray for me and support this ministry. My thanks to Katharina Leipp of Muhlaker, Germany for her friendship and support, and for translating *Caleb's Testimony,* and many articles into the German language. Thanks also to Darren Robinson, for his meticulous assembly of the cover and to Daniel Patrick Landolfi for maintaining the website. But most of all, my heartfelt, humble thanks to our Heavenly Father for His inspiration, guiding hand, protection, and never-ending love. May this work bring joy to His heart and help find that last soul!

"One thing have I

desired of the Lord,

that I will seek after;

that I may dwell

in the house of the Lord

all the days of my life,

to behold the beauty of the Lord,

and to enquire in his temple."

Psalm 27: 4

MESSAGE FROM THE AUTHOR

As we study scripture we must heed the warning found in Revelation 1:19: *"And if any man shall take away from the words of the book of this prophecy, God shall take away his part out of the book of life, and out of the holy city....."*. What this tells us is that we must use the words of scripture as authentically as we can and always regard them as truth. We must check and double check the doctrines under which we sit by comparing them to what scripture tells us. We must work to apply even those things which may be the *perspectives* of the prophets as they relate the visions God allowed them to have. While it is not necessary to our soul salvation to learn about the heavenly hierarchy or the function of angels, it does provide us with a greater understanding of the incredible power which makes up our universe and which ultimately affects everything in our lives. While many disregard scripture, and others believe its words to be only mystical allegories impossible to apply, there are many who *do* believe scripture and use its directives to guide their lives. Those who do trust scripture believe, as I do, that scripture is the word of God given to develop the Bride of Christ and that God will unveil even its most cryptic messages to those who truly desire to learn. In the book titled *"Why Trust Scripture"* in my Why God Why series I presented a variety of information to show how the words of scripture support both the Creation *and* the elements of carbon dating. Interestingly, that information highlighted the fallibility of man's interpretation of scripture and negated any scriptural inconsistency. Another verse which may in time demonstrate the accuracy of scripture and our fallibility in terms of interpretation comes from a vision which the Apostle John was given about the end times. In Revelation 9:3,7,9 and 10 John wrote: *"And there came out of the smoke locusts upon the earth....and the shapes of the locusts were like unto horses prepared unto battle; and on their heads were as it were crowns like gold, and their faces were as the faces of men.....breastplates of iron, and the sound of their wings was as the sound of chariots of many horses....and they had tails like unto scorpions.....and their power was to hurt men five months.*" Some Biblical scholars believe that what John saw in this vision was a fleet of our modern day attack helicopters, while others believe that he saw the demons loosed from the abyss which Revelation 9:11 tells us Isaiah saw in his vision. The Apostle John, never having seen modern technology or this type of demonic activity, could only describe what he saw within the parameters of his limited experience. Nevertheless, those words stand today and are expected to become yet another testament to the perfect accuracy of scripture. Similarly when we read in Revelation 21:21: *"And the twelve gates were twelve pearls....and the street of the city was pure gold...."* we can accept that these words are an attempt to describe the incredible beauty of the city in heaven which will be created for the Bride of Christ. Whether the word "pearl" actually refers to the pearls we find inside a clam or whether it refers to a yet unknown substance which is as white and transparent and shiny as a pearl doesn't really matter. Whether the word gold refers to streets paved with the gold the prophets recognized or with something which is as beautiful and valuable as the gold they referenced also does not matter. What does matter is that we take from scripture those things which teach us about our future and how we can attain the understanding to prepare for that future through the perfection of our soul. Thus, whether allegory or fact, or whether couched in a mystery which is unveiled as we gain a better understanding of God's Plan of Salvation, we can believe that scripture constantly proves itself accurate. Therefore, as we read about angels and seek to understand their role in heaven and how they might impact *our* world, we must look into the words employed by those prophets who described their visions of angels with words found only through their limited perspective. As we study this scripture, we learn that the fallen angels retained the powers they received in heaven and now use those powers *against* mankind. We learn about the theocracy under which we will live and why God requires that everything in the new heaven and earth be free of all things evil. We learn how everything we experience helps us through the growth process we undergo here on earth. We learn to appreciate the plan God has put into place to bring us a new world, free of evil, and filled with a populace who long to live in such an environment. We learn to embrace the breadth of diversity which God has wrought in those things He placed on earth, in heaven, and throughout His universe. We begin to recognize the immensity of God's plan for our future and the love with which He draws us. This helps us grow into a more selfless person with a desire to promote and share that love and an understanding about why we should put on the armour of protection God provides, watch for the influence of fallen angels, and prepare ourselves for the First Resurrection. Therefore, what we can learn about angels and the powers they exert over us, both for good and for bad, will help us spurn the evil whose only goal is to separate us from God to extend its freedom and retain its power. Each of us must make that ever important decision to follow God, avoid Satan's trap of complacency and work to shed the selfish Adam-like nature created when Satan caused Adam and Eve to sin and which we inherited at birth. We must grow into the self-sacrificing Christ-like nature God will look for in the Bride. Therefore, we must learn to recognize the harm the fallen angels seek to do under Satan's directives and can only accomplish this by learning *what* they do and *how* they do it. I hope that you will enjoy this little book and that you will share what you learn with others. May God open your understanding of His words and may He bless you and keep you always.   ***Helen Glowacki***

TABLE OF CONTENTS

"......above all

taking the shield

of faith,

with which you can

quench

all the flaming darts

of the evil one."

Ephesians 6:16

"For we wrestle not against flesh and blood, but against principalities, against powers, against the rulers of the darkness of this world, against spiritual wickedness in high places."
Ephesians 6:12

Chapter One

SPIRITUAL WARFARE

Spiritual warfare is a phrase which we rarely hear, let alone discuss. Yet without our knowledge, every day of our lives, every man, woman, and child is subjected to the battle between God and Satan for their soul. When the angels were created, God endowed them with certain powers and placed them into a hierarchy consisting of three major ranks. Each rank was empowered to perform a specific range of duties. The angels who remained faithful to God use these powers for the good of mankind while the fallen angels use them to harm man and impede his spiritual progress. Few people understand that the fallen angels who followed Satan in his rebellion against God *retained* their powers when they were banished from heaven. Therefore, whether Satan sends a fallen angel to harm us, or God sends a faithful angel to help us, each employ their powers when they interact with or for us. Most angelic interventions are so subtle that we may not recognize their work. Therefore we often do not concern ourselves with the fact that Satan himself, who is the leader of the fallen angels, directs his followers to separate us from God. Satan's desire is to block our awareness that evil is real and active in our lives, and place indifference in our hearts to prevent us from learning about God's plan of salvation. The angels who remain faithful to God help mankind battle these satanic spirits and use their powers to help us learn of God's offer, obtain the forgiveness of sin, and desire, as children of God, to develop into a worthy bride for His Son.

Certain ranks of angels can bring us the gifts of tenderness and hope, of healing and transformation, of various talents and service while the fallen angels pervert these attributes into cruelty and despair, sickness and false doctrines, complacency and selfishness. Thus, scripture teaches us about angels and the work they do; it explains their duties and their powers and describes three spheres of heaven each of which contains three types of angels. The first sphere contains the *Seraphim,* the *Cherubim*, and the *Thrones* who have been given the power to **Counsel.** The second sphere contains the *Dominions*, the *Virtues,* and the *Powers* who have been given the power to **Govern**, and the third sphere contains the *Principalities*, the *Archangels*, and the *Angels* who act as **Messengers.** Rarely do we envision angels as evil, in fact most of us think of angels as beautiful celestial beings emanating an ethereal white light and fashioned with a pair of pure white feathered wings. Some of us think of angels as those sweet beings depicted on a

Valentine's Day card. We envisage angels as immensely attractive, appearing with a God-sent benevolent mission to protect us. But whatever we think angels can or cannot do, we seldom talk about them or study what scripture tells us. Because most people know so little about them they accept what today's culture presents through its variety of venues which fantasize the supernatural, thereby assigning angels to the realm of the fictitious. This prevents us from discussing the fallen angels who bring the evil so rampant here on earth by wielding their incredible power over mankind. Satan has purposely and successfully created an aura of disbelief, even fear, about all things supernatural because he does *not* want us to discuss the mysteries of Heaven. His goal is to encourage the mistaken belief that such discussions are foolish, speculative, and unrealistic in his effort to separate man from God. Yet as we study scripture and learn of God's plan for mankind, we begin to see that all the things of heaven work toward the completion of that plan. We become more convinced than ever of God's all encompassing love for us and the immense power and forethought which went into the Creation and *now* into the separation of good and evil. Through scripture we learn of the angelic hierarchy, and of the duties these angels perform, and through them, gain insight into how heaven may be governed, how a godly theocracy works, and how the perfect order of the elements of our universe are maintained. We also learn that just as God fashioned for *our* world an immense variety of animals, plants, and creatures of the sea, so did God create a variety of angels for the heavens. Scripture teaches us that some angels bear absolutely no resemblance to man and others do. We learn that there are three different orders or spheres in the heavens which mark the distance between heaven and earth and that each sphere contains three different ranks of angels. This tells us that there are nine types of angels. The first order or "sphere" of heaven is that area which is the farthest from earth and is where the throne of God is located. The angels which occupy this sphere have very little resemblance to man and are not seen by man. They were created to surround, protect, praise, and care for the throne of God, the tree of life, Holy places, and the **justice and authority** which God ordains. The second sphere of heaven houses the angels who, while rarely making themselves known to man, use their powers to protect and maintain the **order of the universe.** The third order or sphere contains those angels who are closest to the material world and can manifest themselves to man. They are thought to bring our blessings and to **guard and educate mankind.** Many people believe in angels and many are familiar with those named in the Bible, primarily Michael and Gabriel. But few understand the hierarchy of angels or the duties they perform. Many think of angels only as messengers of God and as those beings assigned to look after mankind. However, while these are the angels most of us are aware of, there are also many angels with different duties and very different characteristics and many who are evil. Years ago a movie titled "Star Wars" was produced which became so popular that additional follow-up movies were created to continue the activities of the prime characters and introduce an even greater variety of "extraterrestrial" characters. Some of these characters were lovable, some funny, some difficult to look at, and others quite a stretch of the imagination. Despite their unusual characteristics, many touched the heart of the viewers and became very popular... and in many cases.... endearing. This occurred because of the personality imbued in that particular extraterrestrial. Sadly, in the case of angels we cannot always fathom their "personality" nor fully understand what work they do for God. Thus, when we read a description of their physical characteristics, we cannot "connect" as we do with the characters in these films. Our idea of what these angels might look like can only be gleaned from the descriptions provided in scripture and can cause us to wonder why God would have given these angels the characteristics He did. But as we learn more about God's creation, we learn how diverse His creation really is. In fact, in recent years explorations of the deeper waters of the seas have brought to light a myriad of creatures which have stunned the world with their unusual forms and incredible intensity of colors. These and other discoveries about that which surrounds us have helped us move toward the understanding that God's creatures, in fact His whole of Creation, are indeed very diverse and that while many of them are beneficial, some, because of sin, are harmful to mankind. As an example, some of the most beautiful plants are the most poisonous to man while some of the least impressive plants have gifted us with amazing healing properties. Therefore, as we read about angels and their diverse duties and characteristics we better understand the different characteristics and duties of man, flora and fauna in our personal environment. We also understand the dilemma of the prophets when writing scripture and describing those things which were unfamiliar to them. They were in fact often frightened by their visions and could only write into scripture what their limited perspectives allowed. Scripture tells us that angels come in many different forms and are very diverse in appearance. Some, those who we simply know as "angels" or perhaps our "guardian" angel, are described as having the form, face and limbs of mankind, some with wings and others without wings. But these are only one of the nine types of angels and the ones who, more often than not, present themselves to man in the form which we can readily accept and recognize. While there are different schools of thought about angels, as mentioned previously, it is generally believed that there are nine types of angels, residing in three different spheres of heaven, who are responsible for carrying out three major duties. To carry out these duties the angels have been endowed with the powers required to do so. Purportedly, those angels who have the closest proximity to man are located in the third sphere of heaven which is the closest to earth. These are the angels who are the most familiar to us. Scripture identifies the three types of angels in this sphere as the **Principalities**, (also known as *"rulers"*), the **Archangels** and the **Angels**. Their duty is to act as Heaven's messengers. The second sphere of heaven is located further from our material world and contains those angels who operate as Heaven's governors. They are the **Dominions**, the **Virtues** and the **Powers**. The Powers are also known in scripture as the *Authorities*. The first sphere of Heaven which is closest to God and farthest from earth contains the Heavenly counselors. These angels are called the **Seraphim**, the **Cherubim** and the **Thrones** (who are also known, but not through scripture, as the *Ophanim*). Both those angels who remain faithful to God, and those who joined Satan's rebellion against God, continue to have and use the powers with which they were created.

"After these things I saw four angels standing on the four corners of the earth, holding the four winds of the earth, that the wind should not blow on the earth, nor on the sea, nor on any tree."
Revelation 7:1

Chapter Two

THE SERAPHIM

The highest ranking angels are the four Seraphim whose powers include those as Heavenly counselors. They are described in Revelation 4:6-8. The first Seraph is said to have a face which resembles a lion, the second a face which resembles a calf, the third a face which resembles a man, and the fourth a face which resembles a flying eagle. They have a human-like form with hands and feet, possess many eyes, give constant glory, honor and thanks to God, and circle the throne upon which

God sits. (Isaiah 6:2) The many eyes which these angels possess indicate that these angels see the entire universe and watch what God oversees. The prophet Isaiah was given a vision in which he saw these Seraphim, describing each as having six wings; two to cover their face, two to cover their feet, and two with which to fly. Without stopping day or night, they cried to one another the words, *"Holy, holy, holy, is the Lord of hosts; the whole earth is full of his glory."* In Isaiah's vision, one of them flew to him bringing him a live coal which the Seraph had taken off the altar with a tong. He offered the coal to Isaiah with his hand. (Isaiah 6:6) God asked Isaiah who He could send to the people to teach them and Isaiah answered by offering to go himself. (Isaiah 6:8) God told Isaiah that the people heard, but they did not understand, and they saw, yet they did not perceive. (Isaiah 6:9) God provided Isaiah with this vision so he could warn the people of what was to come and to convince the people of the need to repent and learn of and follow God's precepts. Most scholars believe that Isaiah's vision was of the end times. In this vision, Isaiah saw a book covered by seven seals which could only be opened by Christ because He was the only one worthy to do so. When Christ opened the book to loose these seven seals, the Seraphim and twenty four elders holding harps and vials filled with the prayers of the saints, fell down before Him. They sang a new song saying: *"Thou art worthy to take the book, and to open the seals thereof; for thou wast slain, and hast redeemed us to God by thy blood out of every kindred, and tongue, and nation.; and hast made us unto our God kings and priests; and we shall reign on earth."* (Revelation 5: 8-10) Isaiah saw many angels around the throne who joined the Seraphim and the elders, and altogether they numbered over **one hundred million.** (Revelation 5:11) When the Seraphim said *"Amen"*, one of the four told Isaiah to come closer so he could see what occurred when Christ loosed the first seal. Isaiah then saw a man on a white horse who wore a crown and carried a bow, and "went forth **conquering and to conquer**". The second Seraph told Isaiah to *"Come and see"* as the second seal loosed a red horse whose rider was sent to **remove peace from the earth**. The third Seraph bade Isaiah to *"Come and see"* as a black horse carried a rider with a pair of balances in his hand to **ration food**. The fourth Seraph told Isaiah to *"Come and see"* as a pale horse carried a rider who was given the power to bring **death and hell** to the earth. The fifth and sixth and seventh seals were also opened and Isaiah saw the saints calling to God and then saw the final desolation which was so devastating that **every mountain was moved out of its place** and men hid themselves in fear. After this, Isaiah saw four angels standing at the four corners of the earth and another angel calling to them telling them to hold back the final destruction **until all the servants of God were sealed.** Twelve thousand souls from each of the twelve tribes of Israel were clothed in white robes and were sealed, and Isaiah was told that they were those who had washed their robes in the blood of Christ and would dwell with God forever. Then the seventh seal was opened and seven angels with seven trumpets stood before God while another came into their presence holding a censer filled with fire which he threw to the earth. As each angel sounded their trumpet, another terrible desolation occurred on earth. A fifth angel was given the key to the bottomless pit and told to open it to allow the demons from that abyss to be released upon the earth so they could bring mankind great torment. (Revelation 9:11). For the next five months, smoke, pestilence and **torment came forth to torture those left** on earth and men wished for death and could not find it. (Revelation 9:3, 5) Then the sixth angel sounded his trumpet and four angels bound in the Euphrates River were loosed and brought an army of two million who **killed one third of all mankind** with fire, brimstone and smoke which issued from the horses they rode. Despite all this, the people did not repent of the wrong they had done in the sight of God. Isaiah saw another angel sent to seal those things which the seven thunders uttered and to proclaim that *there would be time no longer because now the mystery of God was finished.* This is when God's plan to develop the Bride will be complete. Then Isaiah was told to go forth to prophesy and tell the people what he saw so that they would repent. God asked Him to bring his vision before many peoples and nations, and tongues and kings. We learn from these verses that God holds the power to completely destroy this earth and everything in it and that some of these powers have been imbued into angels who do as God bids them to do. Thus God holds back the destruction of our earth until those souls whom God longs for will be made ready for the First Resurrection through their faith and the forgiveness of sin. It also shows us that the fallen angels use their powers to harm mankind in the mistaken belief that they can delay the completion of God's plan.

"So he drove out man; and he placed at the east of the garden of Eden Cherubims and a flaming sword which turned every way to keep the way of the tree of life." Genesis 3:24

Chapter Three

THE CHERIBIM

Scripture depicts Cherubs as mighty and fearsome four winged beasts with four faces (Ezekiel 10:14) and usually mention them as pairs. 1 Kings 6:24-26 describes them as ten cubits tall with a ten cubit wing span. A cubit is approximately eighteen inches long which means that their wings and height are approximately fifteen feet. They are mentioned in Genesis, Exodus, Numbers, Ezekiel, Isaiah, Kings, Chronicles, Samuel 1 and 2, in Psalms, and in Hebrews. When scripture describes these angels it is usually for the purpose of creating a likeness of them to place in the tabernacle and on the mercy seat of the Ark of the Covenant where they act as a protector of that which is holy. We can read in Ezekiel 10:21 that the Cherubim have four wings, (as opposed to the six wings of the Seraphim). They have straight feet similar to that of a calf, and hands like that of a man under their wings. Scripture describes what the artisans were told to do to create a likeness of the cherubim for the adorning of the Tabernacle and the Ark of the Covenant. The artisans were to create two cherubim whose wings would touch one another and also touch each wall of the tabernacle. These carvings were to be ten cubits high, made from olive wood and covered with gold. (1 Kings 6:23-28) The walls were also to be decorated with carvings of Cherubs and of carvings of palm trees and open flowers. Exodus 25:10-11 tells us that Moses was instructed to create an ark of testimony about 45" long, 27" wide and 27" high from Shittim wood, and to overlay it with gold. The Cherubim were to flank each end and stretch forth their wings over the mercy seat. Their faces were to look toward one another over the seat thereby watching and protecting what was between them. (Exodus 25:21) God told Moses that it was at this mercy seat where God would commune with him, and through him He would command the people of Israel. (Exodus 25:22) These instructions, and therefore how the Cherubim are used, indicates that these angels are commissioned to look after the Holy things of God and act as protectors of those things which God ordains as Holy. Psalm 80:1 tells us: *"Give ear, O Shepherd of Israel, thou that leadest Joseph like a flock; thou that dwellest between the cherubims, shine forth."* This verse again is indicative of the cherubim being assigned to guard a special place where those who love God gather and act in accordance with God's will. If the people did as God instructed it would place them under God's protection through the watchful eyes of the Cherubim. Scripture also tells us that wheels very similar to chariot wheels are usually found with, on, or near the Cherubim. Ezekiel 10:6-10 tells us *".....Take fire from between the wheels from between the cherubims; then he went in, and stood beside the wheels. And one cherub stretched forth his hand from between the cherubims unto the fire that was between the cherubims, and took thereof, and put it into the hands of him that was clothed with linen: who took it and went out. And there appeared in the cherubims, the form of a man's hand under their wings. And when I looked, behold the four wheels by the cherubims, one wheel by one cherub, and another wheel by another cherub; and the appearance of the wheels was as the colour of a beryl stone. And as for their appearances, they four had one likeness, as if a wheel had been in the midst of a wheel."* And in Ezekiel 10:16 we can read: *"And when the cherubims went, the wheels went by them: and when the cherubims lifted up their wings to mount up from the earth, the same wheels also turned not from beside them."* Ezekiel 10:19 adds: *And the cherubims lifted up their wings, and mounted up from the earth in my sight: when they went out, the wheels also were beside them, and every one stood at the door of the east gate of the Lord's house; and the glory of the God of Israel was over them above."* These verses indicate that the duty of the Cherubim is to protect what God put into place for those who love Him. These include God's temple, house, ark, tree of life, garden and children. The wheels, often described in connection with the Cherubim may be another type of angel....the Thrones. Scripture teaches that we do not fully grasp the many warnings God has given us and tells us in Hosea 4:6: *"My people are destroyed for lack of knowledge; because thou hast rejected knowledge, I will also reject thee, that thou shall be no priest to me: seeing thou hast forgotten the law of thy God, I will also forget thy children."* This verse and others explain that without an understanding of scripture, we cannot learn how to commune with God, how to thank Him, or how to battle evil. As we learn about the incredible evil which comes from the fallen angels, we are inspired to work harder for our soul salvation. Revelation 9: 1-11, 11:7-8 and 13:1 refers to the "beast" who some scholars believe is Abbadon a powerful fallen angel who will, during the end times, be loosed from the bottomless pit with his kingdom of demons to rule over earth and cause incredible torment to mankind. His power will last for forty-two months (Revelation 13:5, 11:13 and Daniel 7:25, 12:7) However, through scripture we find that God explains every facet of the provisions He has made for us, and is fully aware of the battles we face. God tells us how to find favor with Him and what protection He offers from a world filled with evil. He teaches us what He plans for those who love Him and do their best to follow His precepts. He also tells us that the Bride of Christ will be taken at the First Resurrection and escape that part of the end times when these demons are released.

"I fell down to worship before the feet of the angel which shewed me these things. Then saith he unto me: See thou do not do it..." **Revelation 22: 8-9**

Chapter Four

THE THRONES

The Thrones are those angels who are generally listed as the third category of angels in the First Sphere. They, like the Seraphim and Cherubim, are considered to be the highest ranking angels and thus have the closest proximity to God. They, like the Seraphim and Cherubim, are believed to dispense justice, to point out injustice, and to maintain all universal laws. They carry out these duties with perfect objectivity. Colossians 1:16 tells us: *"For by him were all things created, that are in heaven, and that are in earth, visible and invisible, whether they be thrones or dominions, or principalities or powers; all things were created by him, and for him.*" This verse in Colossians lists four of the nine categories of angels. Additionally, since the word "throne" also refers to the actual throne of God and also to the thrones of those who govern here on earth, it can be difficult to discern the scripture which refers to these angels. There are however, no scriptural references to the word Ophanim, which is another name for the Thrones. The word Ophanim is plural and is the Hebrew word for wheels. Since the Cherubim are so closely associated with great circular wheels, special care must be taken to differentiate between these two groups of angels. This is why both the Cherubim and the Thrones are believed to work together. In fact, Ezekiel 10-17 says: *"When they moved, the others moved' when they stopped, the others stopped; and when they rose from the earth, the wheels rose along with them......*" This indicates that both types of angels work in harmony with one another. The Ophanim, though not mentioned in scripture are, according to Wikipedia, first mentioned in the book of Enoch. Here they are described as a celestial being which eternally stands watch over God's throne, burn with a bright glowing heavenly light or eternal flame, and are sometimes depicted as the actual chariots of God driven by the Cherubs. The rims of their wheels are full of eyes with which they can see the entire universe. Thus this description fits closely to what scripture says about Thrones. Other references depict these angels as "Ofanim, Wheels of Galgallin". It is generally believed that Daniel 7:9-10 is describing the Thrones when stating: *"....his throne was like the fiery flame, and his wheels as burning fire. A fiery stream issued and came forth from before him.......the judgment was set, and the books were opened."* We can therefore conclude that the three ranks of angels who reside in the first sphere of heaven attend to God, to His Holy seat in heaven, and carefully watch what God oversees. As we read about the angels in this first sphere of heaven, it does not appear that any of these angels followed Satan. It also is *not* mentioned in scripture that they appear to man other than in a God granted vision. As we contemplate the majesty and power and duties of the angels we can understand why scripture clearly warns us not to worship angels or any of the host of heaven. This includes the sun and the moon and the stars. Scripture tells us that to do so is an abomination to God. Understanding the powers of the angels helps us understand how those powers can be used to pull us away from God even through a seemingly innocent interest in astrology. According to scripture the use of astrology is deemed the worshipping of other gods. Deuteronomy 17:3-5 explains: *"And hath gone and served other gods, and worshipped them, either the sun, or moon, or any of the host of heaven which I have not commanded. And it be told thee, and thou has heard of it, and inquired diligently, and behold, it be true, and the thing certain that such abomination is wrought.....*" Deuteronomy 4:19 warns: *"And lest thou lift up thine eyes unto heaven and when thou seest the sun, and the moon, and the stars, even all the host of heaven, shouldst be driven to worship them, and serve them, which the Lord thy God hath divided unto all nations under the whole heaven."* Colossians 2:18 warns: *"Let no man beguile you of your reward in a voluntary humility and worshipping of angels, intruding into those things which he hath not seen, vainly puffed up by his fleshly mind."* And Revelation 22:8-9 tells us: *".....And when I had heard and seen, I fell down to worship before the feet of the angel which shewed me these things. Then saith he unto me, See thou do not do it; for I am thy fellowservant, and of thy brethren the prophets, and of them which keep the saying of this book; worship God."* As we read scripture, we begin to learn of the incredible majesty of God and all He has put into place to execute His plan of salvation for us. But we also learn what pleases and displeases God so that we can grow into those He wants for His new kingdom. Proverbs 3:8 tells us that to know and acknowledge God is *"...health to thy navel, and marrow to thy bones."* Proverbs 3:3-6 tells us, *"Let not mercy and truth forsake thee; bind them about thy neck; write them upon the table of thine heart. So shalt thou find favor and good understanding in the sight of God and man. Trust in the Lord with all thine heart; and lean not to your own understanding. In all thy ways, acknowledge him and he shall direct thy paths."* Therefore, despite the power and majesty of the angels and the understanding of their duties as outlined in scripture, we know to worship *only* God just as He told us to do in the Ten Commandments. We develop a better understanding of what God means when He tells us not to worship "other gods". We also learn that just as we are asked to serve our fellowman, the angels are asked to serve God, and in doing so, to also serve us.

"Then opened he their understanding that they might understand the scriptures."
Luke 24:45

Chapter Five

THE DOMINIONS

The angels who are known as the Dominions occupy the second sphere of heaven and are one of three ranks of angels whose duties and powers are that of Heavenly governors. They are believed to resemble divinely beautiful humans, have one pair of feathered wings and carry a scepter or a sword from which emanates an orb of light. Dominions are believed to regulate the duties of the lower angels and to preside over nations. The word "dominions" however is used only twice in scripture: Colossians 1:16 tells us: *"For by him* *were all things created, that are in heaven, and that are in earth, visible and invisible, whether they be thrones, or **dominions**.......*" And Daniel 7:27 tells us*: "And the kingdom and dominion, and the greatness of the kingdom under the whole of heaven, shall be given to the people of the saints of the most High, whose kingdom is an everlasting kingdom, and all **dominions** shall serve and obey him."* The word "dominion" however is mentioned sixty two times in scripture but refers to ownership more often than to angels. However, Ephesians 1:21 does use the word dominion to describe this rank of angels. When Christ was raised from the dead and given a seat at God's right hand in the heavenly places, scripture tells us that He was "far above" the angels and specifically mentions the angels in the second and third sphere of heaven. *"Far above all principality, and power, and might, and **dominion,** and every name that is named, not only in this world, but also in that which is to come."* Dominions and Powers are two of the three ranks of angels in this second sphere of heaven while the Principalities are in the third sphere. Scripture does not refer to any of the angels in the first sphere....the Seraphim, Cherubim or Thrones....as those who help Satan harm the children of God, but does name the lower ranks of angels. This supports the conclusion that it is from the second and third sphere that Satan drew those angels who joined his rebellion and that possibly no Seraphim, Cherubim or Thrones followed Satan. Since Dominions are associated with having power over nations, it is thought that when Daniel referred to "a wicked spiritual power" which controlled Persia (Daniel 10:12-13) he may have been referring to a Dominion angel. While the "Powers" and the "Principalities" are most often mentioned by name, inference is made to other ranks through the words "rulers of darkness" and "spiritual wickedness in high places". Ephesians 6:12 says: *"For we wrestle not against flesh and blood, but against principalities, against powers, against the rulers of the darkness of this world, against spiritual wickedness in high places.* " While it is not clear which rank Satan held, it appears that all the angels have access to God and His throne. Tobit 12:15 states: *"I am Raphael, one of the seven holy angels. Which present the prayers of the saints, and which go in and go out before the glory of the Holy One."* Raphael is an archangel from the third sphere of heaven, thus we can assume from this passage and others that *all* angels have this access to God. It is believed by some scholars that Satan was the chief of the Powers when he was cast from heaven. Others believe that he was of the rank of the Seraphim, and others a Cherub, but whatever his rank, Satan's power over mankind is clearly explained. Scripture warns that Satan has the power to move men to do his bidding (1 Chronicles 21:1), to walk back and forth on the earth (Job 1:7), to cause illness (Job 2:7), to take God's word from men's hearts (Mark 4:15), to enter man (Luke 22:3), to blind the minds of them which believe not (John

13:27), to transform himself (2 Corinthians 4:4), to send messengers to hurt man (2 Corinthians 11:14), to hinder people (2 Corinthians 12:7), to produce signs and has powers (1 Thessalonians 2:18), and to use his power to convince man to accept his perversions. (2 Thessalonians 2:9). Satan also uses *mankind* to perpetrate his evil, separate us from God and pervert the Gospel of Christ. He can infiltrate the hearts of men to pervert scripture enough to blind the eyes of men to the correct interpretation. An example of this is found in the doctrine of Collective Salvation/Redemption which promotes covetousness and envy through the redistribution of wealth. Satan also directs the fallen angels to influence those who *govern* this world. Thus we find evil and corruption, attacks on Christians and Christianity infusing even our present governing bodies. This is why we are urged to pray for God's protection and ask the Holy Spirit to guide us. We can request the angel protection in what we do and think so we can be a blessing and never perpetrate

Satan's deceptions. Luke 24:45 tells us, *"Then opened he their understanding, that they might understand the scriptures."* 1 Corinthians 2: 10, tells us, *"But God hath revealed them to us by his Spirit; for the Spirit searcheth all things, yea, the deep things of God."* Luke 12:12 says, *"For the Holy Ghost shall teach you . . ".* The Apostle Paul, who was also given the ability to understand the mysteries of God, wrote in Ephesians 3:3,4,8,9, *"How that by revelation he made known unto me the mystery; (.....Whereby, when ye read, ye may understand my knowledge in the mystery of Christ) Which in other ages was not made known unto the sons of men, as it is now revealed unto his holy apostles and prophets by the Spirit.........Unto me, who am less than the least of all saints, is this grace given, that I should preach among the Gentiles the unsearchable riches of Christ; And to make all men see what is the fellowship of the mystery, which from the beginning of the world hath been hid in God, who created all things by Christ Jesus."*

> *"Far above all principality, and power, and might, and dominion, and every name that is named, not only in this world, but also in that which is to come."* Ephesians 1:21

Chapter Six

VIRTUES

The angels known as the "Virtues" reside in the second sphere of heaven. It is believed that when scripture uses the words "strong" "strongholds" or "might" in reference to angels, it is the Virtues to which those words apply. Revelation 5:2 tells us: *"And I saw a **strong** angel proclaiming with a loud voice...."* And Ephesians 1:21 tells us: *"Far above all principality, and power, and **might,** and dominion, and every name that is named, not only*

in this world, but also in that which is to come."
The words, Principality, Power and Dominion are all references to specific ranks of angels, thus the position of the word "might" most likely indicates a rank of angels who fall between the other two. Thus, the placement of this word between the word "dominion" and the word "power" would indicate that this word most likely refers to the Virtues.

The Virtues are also known as "The Brilliant or Shining Ones" because they are associated with the duty to preside over celestial life and supervise the movements of the heavenly bodies. Also attributed to this rank of angels is the control of the elements, of nature, and of the seasons, as well as the stars, moon, and the sun. This had led some scholars to believe that the Virtues who joined Satan's rebellion became those who seduce man into trusting the predictions of astrologers, and disobeying God through their practice of the occult which is, as previously mentioned, the "worship" of "other gods". However, the Virtues who remained faithful to God are thought to help us grow in holiness, watch over us, work miracles on earth, and stay closely connected to the saints. Apparently, they are also the angels who hold the elements in check and keep them from destroying the earth. We can read in Revelation 7:1: *"And after these things I saw four angels standing on the four corners of the earth, holding the four winds of the earth, that the wind should not blow on the earth, nor on the sea, nor on any tree."* And in Revelation 7:3 we can read: *"Saying, Hurt not the earth, neither the sea, nor the trees, til we have sealed the servants of our God in their foreheads."* Interestingly, scripture tells us that on many occasions when an angel visited mankind, those to whom they spoke were not immediately aware that they spoke to an angel. An example of this is found in Judges 13:16: *".......For Manoah knew **not** that he was an angel of the Lord"*. And in verse 21: *".....Then Manoah knew that he **was** an angel of the Lord."* Hebrews

13:2 tells us: *Be not forgetful to entertain strangers; for thereby some have entertained angels* **unawares.**" There are also verses in scripture which describe the manner in which angels are sent to help us and to act against those who persecute God's children and disobey God. Psalms 34:7 tells us: *"The angel of the Lord encampeth round them.......and* **delivereth** *them."* And Psalm 35:5 says: *"Let them be as chaff before the wind; and let the angel of the Lord* **chase** *them."* And in Psalm 35:6: *"Let their way be dark and slippery; and let the angel of the Lord* **persecute** *them."* Acts 12:23 warns: *"And immediately the angel of the Lord* **smote** *him, because he gave not God the glory; and he was eaten of worms, and gave up the ghost."* While there seems to be no direct statement that these are the angels who work to instill in mankind the many virtues God wants us to develop such as kindness and honor, faith and truthfulness, etc., many believe that this *is* a part of the work they do for God. Conversely then, the fallen angels in this rank would work to create malice, dishonor, faithlessness, and a lying nature to name a few. As we read of angels and the work the faithful angels do for God and for mankind we are reminded that we are fallible. If we arrogantly believe that we already know all there is to know and need only to believe and not *work* toward our soul salvation, we shortchange our spiritual growth and can succumb to the work of the fallen angels. As we increase our knowledge about God's creation, the Holy Spirit can increase in us as well and can liberate us from the fallen angels who are the spirits of this world working to separate us from the fullness of God's truths and protection. Scripture also teaches us to *prove* what we hear and what we read by comparing it to what God tells us through His words in scripture. We are warned never to trust only in the wisdom of men, but to compare their words to the words God has given us. Perhaps we cannot always or immediately understand the words of scripture or place them into their proper perspective, but we *can* test what we hear by checking them against scripture and asking God to clarify His words. If what we read and hear and do, brings love and joy, peace and longsuffering, gentleness, goodness and faith, and employs meekness and temperance, is supported by scripture, and reveres the teaching of Christ then we *can* trust those words. When this is our desire God will bless us and help us learn. The Apostle Paul wrote in Romans 8:38: *"For I am persuaded that neither death, nor life, nor **angels, nor principalities, nor powers,** nor things present, nor things to come……shall be able to separate us from the love of God which is in Christ Jesus our Lord."* The Apostles' use of the words "angels, principalities and powers" refers to three of the different ranks of angels who joined Satan's rebellion against God and are thus the fallen angels. Not all angels in these ranks followed Satan therefore many remain faithful to God and provide the godly influence to mankind which God has so lovingly provided for us.

"Be sober, be vigilant, because your adversary the devil, as a roaring lion, walketh about, seeking who he may devour."
1 Peter 5:8

Chapter Seven

POWERS

Scripture tells us that before Satan rebelled against God he was called Lucifer and was the most beautiful angel in heaven. He waged war against God hoping to prevent God from elevating man to a position higher than the angels. His beauty and power, and his desire to stop God's plan and become a ruler in heaven drew one third of all the angels to join his rebellion. He rebelled because of his jealousy toward Christ, toward mankind, and toward God's plan for them, and was thus banned from Heaven. Some scholars believe that Satan was the chief of all angels assigned to the rank of the Powers. Most believe that it is he who is referenced by the words "ruler of the darkness of this world", and he and his fallen angels who are referenced by the words "spiritual wickedness in high places". Ephesians 2:2 also speaks of Satan with the words: *"Wherein in time past ye walked according to the* **prince of the power**, *the spirit that now worketh in the children of disobedience."* A prince or ruler usually has the support of an army who does as he bids, thus this verse seems to indicate that many of those in Satan's army were angels in the rank of the Powers. Luke 11:15 tells us that Beelzebub (Satan) is the chief of devils and has authority over all the demons who work on his behalf to break the faith of God's children. When Satan and his followers waged war against God, they were overcome and were thrown out of heaven to the earth. Thus, Satan and all the angels who joined his rebellion became the demons here on earth who work to prevent man from learning of and obeying God. These angels realize that if man disobeys God just as they did, no man, they reason, could reside with God and therefore God's plan of salvation could not be completed. They believe that delaying the completion of God's plan allows them to retain their power in the earthly kingdom over which Satan currently reigns, and escape punishment for their rebellion. Scripture tells us that their punishment is to be bound into the Lake of Fire for all eternity. Thus Satan tempted Adam and Eve to sin, and the fallen angels who followed Satan and retained the powers of their rank, began to use those powers against mankind to prevent God's plan of salvation from being completed. Nevertheless, God's plan does move forward and *will* be completed. Thus, at some point, *every* fallen angel who harmed God's children will be thrown into the Lake of Fire with Satan and with them will be those of mankind who choose not to follow God. They will remain in hell for all eternity and be forever separated from God. They will be *continuously* tormented by hatred, anger, envy, jealousy, back biting, cruelty, lies, slander and all things evil. To thwart Satan's plan, God gave man the scriptures so they could learn about Satan and the fallen angels and learn of the sacrifice Christ made which paid the ransom demanded by man's sin. Scripture clearly warns that these powerful fallen angels bring sin to mankind to retain their freedom and do so with a vengeance, desperately trying to delay the completion of God's plan and thus delay when they will be bound forever. Scripture also teaches us how to fight the sin with which Satan and his demons tempt us. Ephesians 6:11-12 tells us: *"Put on the whole armour of God, that ye may be able to* ***stand against the wiles of the devil.*** *For we wrestle not against flesh and blood but against principalities, against powers, against the rulers of the darkness of this world, against spiritual wickedness in high places."* In Luke 11:20-22, we are told that God is more powerful than Satan and that God has given His Apostles the power to cast these devils out of man. However, Luke 24-26 warns that these spirits can come back and re-enter man if he does not *truly* repent and that they can fill our soul with ungodly endeavors which can force the Holy Spirit to leave. Even Christ makes mention of the powerful position which Satan holds in our world by calling him a prince when speaking about his eventual demise. In John 12:31 Christ tells us: *"Now is the judgment of this world, now shall **the prince of this world** be cast out."* God, out of His perfect love and understanding, knows that Satan and those who follow him work to tempt us to sin, thus God offers to forgive our sins. The pre-requisites for that forgiveness are that we *acknowledge* our sins, have *remorse* for them, *strive* not to commit those sins again, and that we willingly *forgive* others. Therefore as Satan works to cause us to sin, he also works to make us forget to acknowledge not only the sins we have *committed* but also those sins of *omission* which are the actions God asks us to take which we do not take. Scripture, God's direct instruction and comfort, presents every nuance of God's plan for mankind and how Satan works to prevent that plan from being completed. It teaches us to look *inward* so we can spurn those attacks and watch for even those seven deadly sins which are so hard to discern. It teaches us why it is necessary to learn God's words, and strive to understand all that He wants to tell us. As God's words unfold and we recognize the qualities required in those God wants for His kingdom, we realize that we have much to learn. We must adjust our thoughts and actions to God's words, shed our old nature and become more loving, more giving, more understanding, and take on the Christ-like nature God longs for. But if we don't know all the little parts which make up the whole, we do not have the tools by which we can grow into that nature, nor know how to recognize the work of Satan and his followers. Nor will we understand that his followers unleash natural disasters, cause unrest in families and inspire evil in our leaders to cause man to believe that there is no God who can or will control such activity. The Holy Spirit can help us fully understand these mysteries, avoid satanic traps, recognize our sins, and desire forgiveness. I Peter 3:22 tells us: *"Who is gone into heaven, And is on the right hand of God; angels and authorities and powers being made subject unto him."* This teaches us that Christ holds ultimate power over the angels. 1 Peter 5:8 says, *"Be sober, be vigilant, because your **adversary the devil,** as a roaring lion, walketh about, seeking who he may devour."* Hebrews 8:12 tells us, *"For I will be merciful to their unrighteousness, and their sins and their iniquities will I remember no more."* Hebrews 10:14, 17 also tell us, *"For by one offering he hath perfected for ever them that are sanctified. And their sins and iniquities will I remember no more."* As these end times are fulfilled, God warns in Mark 13:20: *"And except that the Lord hath shortened, those days, **no flesh should be saved;***

but for the elect's sake, whom he hath chosen, he hath shortened them." God wants us to value love, trust, and loyalty, and to practice these attributes *voluntarily* and tap into the power which the sacrifice of Christ affords the children of God. (John 14:23) Colossians 1:13 tells us that the triumph of Christ *"....hath **delivered us from the power of darkness,** and hath translated us into the kingdom of His dear Son."* Christ could have overpowered the evil forces which brought Him before those who crucified Him, but Romans 13:1-7 explains that God allowed those satanic forces to exercise their power to fulfill the words of scripture and execute the prophecies foretelling the sacrifice of Christ. As we learn, we are strengthened. We see that God ultimately controls everything and gave authority to the Powers to influence those who govern us so prophecy would be fulfilled. The fallen angels exercise these same powers but to produce evil....and only because God allows their activity to bring about the end times.

> *"My people are destroyed for lack of knowledge; because thou hast rejected knowledge, I will also reject thee....."*
> *Hosea 4:6*

Chapter Eight

PRINCIPALITIES

The Principalities are one of the ranks of angels who exist in the third sphere of heaven and are thus in the sphere which is the closest to our world. The three ranks of angels found in this sphere have been tasked with the duty of being Heavenly Messengers. They are usually depicted as wearing a crown and carrying a scepter and are believed to have been created by God not only to be messengers, but to inspire mankind in the arts and sciences. They were created for Christ and through Christ to help spread the gospel. (Colossians 1:16) However, the Principalities which joined Satan's rebellion and now follow Satan work *against* the spread of the gospel. They also *pervert* that gospel hoping to postpone the completion of God's plan of salvation and thus postpone their punishment. The good news is that two thirds of all the angels which God created **remain faithful** to God and thereby to Christ. 1 Peter 3:22 tells us that Christ *"....is gone into heaven and is on the right hand of God, angels and authorities and powers being subject to Him."* And Colossians 2:10 tells us that Christ is *".....the head of all principality and power."* Additionally, Christ told His apostles that He gave **to them** the *"....power of the enemy, and nothing shall by any means hurt you."* (Luke 10:19) Further, Christ's triumph on the cross and His subsequent resurrection not only freed mankind from the hold which Satan had on him, but also hurt the authority of the principalities and powers. Colossians 2:15

says: *"And having* **spoiled** *principalities and powers, he made a shew of them openly,* **triumphing** *over them in it."* It is generally believed that just as the angels who are still in heaven are a part of a hierarchal structure, so are the fallen angels here on earth bound by a hierarchal structure. Scripture tells us that Satan is the ruler of the fallen angels and that his kingdom of angels is referred to as the kingdom of darkness here on earth and that they work day and night to break and pervert the faith of the children of God. In fact, Ephesians 6:12 uses the words: *"rulers of the darkness of this world"* to describe the performers in this effort. As mentioned previously however, those who adhere to the teachings of Christ can overcome those spirits through the power imbued in them by His sacrifice. But those who have *not* placed Christ first in their heart automatically allow the activity of these fallen angels to overcome them and influence their thoughts and actions. These fallen angels are the antagonistic authority over our world and exhibit supernatural abilities so powerful that they can influence people, cities, and even nations. For example, Daniel 10:13 describes a wicked spiritual power which controlled the ancient nation of Persia. In Daniel 10:12 we are told of the angel who answered Daniel's prayer to help Israel. This angel told Daniel that his prayer had been heard and acted upon as soon as he brought his prayer to God, *but* that the angel was delayed in responding because *"the prince of the kingdom of Persia withstood me one and twenty days, but Michael, one of the five chief princes came to help me....."* The words "prince of the kingdom of Persia" refers to the satanic ruler of the spiritual kingdom of darkness which controlled the nation of Persia. This satanic prince was so powerful that he could delay God's messenger until an archangel came to rescue him. However, there are also angels from the ranks of the Principalities who operate here on earth who *are* from God and are *not* a part of the satanic or fallen angels. The Principality who spoke with Daniel was one such angel who *was* faithful to God but **whose powers were not strong enough to fight the Prince of Darkness** who governed Persia. Therefore, the archangel warrior named Michael came to help him. Daniel's prayers acted as the catalyst which caused the angels to come with their help. The angel told Daniel *"I have come for thy words."* This verse in scripture shows us how powerful our prayers are and teaches us that we can call upon the angel protection. It also tells us that as children of God we must constantly battle the forces of evil but that our prayers are very powerful in helping us in this task. We also learn that Christ gave the church the authority to bind those spirits. Matthew 16:18-19 assures us: *"And I say also unto thee, That thou art Peter, and upon this rock I will build my church; and the gates of* ***hell shall not prevail*** *against it. And I will give unto thee the keys of the kingdom of heaven; and whatsoever thou shalt bind on earth shall be bound in heaven; and whatsoever thou shalt loose on earth* *shall be loosed in heaven."* As we read these passages and begin to understand the power used to bring spiritual harm to man, we realize that it is important to understand why Satan does what he does and how we can withstand the power he employs to work his evil. John 8:44 speaks of Satan, saying: *"...... for he is a liar and the father of it."* And in John 8:44, *"........He was a murderer from the beginning, and abode not in the truth, because there is no truth in him......"* This clearly indicates that we must be on guard against the lies evil tells which distract us from the goal of our faith which is to remain faithful to God and become a part of the Bride of His Son. Satan loves the anonymity of working in secret to keep us from God. He wants us to hate and judge and condemn... not him, but other souls. He is so subtle that many cannot believe that he exists, or that his fallen angels bring such harm. Genesis 3:1 tells us, *"..... the serpent was more subtil than any beast......"* These verses teach us that Satan is a liar, a murderer (of men's souls), and is subtle in his attacks. Matthew 4:1 adds that Satan also tempts us and calls him "the tempter". *"Then was Jesus led...... to be tempted of the devil."* And in Matthew 4: 3 *"and when the tempter came to Him, he said....."* Thus we know that Satan has power, is unscrupulous, and wants to separate us from God; we know that the fallen angels who work with Satan also tempt and lie and are subtle in their attacks. As we read scripture, the beautiful plan which begins and ends with God's desire for the future of mankind is unveiled. Scripture explains that God, knowing man would sin, arranged for him to learn of good and evil so he would have the opportunity to recognize the wiles of Satan, freely choose good, repent of all evil, and thereby seek the forgiveness of sin, and a life with God. Scripture teaches us that God longs to fill His kingdom with souls who will truly love *one another*, and love His Son and Him above all else. God began His plan by creating the earth in its limited universe and then created Adam and Eve to live happily in the Garden of Eden, walking and talking with Him. But the angel Lucifer, later known as Satan, rebelled against God because he was jealous of Christ, and of the new being, man, who God planned to elevate above the angels. (Isaiah 14:12-15) As a result of his rebellion, Satan was thrown to earth with the angels who followed him and thereby also disobeyed God. (Revelation 12:9) These numbered one-third of all the angels. Satan knew God's plan and understood that when the plan was completed, and God had obtained the number of faithful loving souls He longed for, Satan would be thrown into Hell for what he had done and with him *all* evil would be forever bound. To prevent God's plan from moving forward and thus forestall his own destruction, Satan destroyed God's relationship of trust and loyalty with Adam and Eve by enticing them to sin through disobedience. Satan knew that sin would automatically separate man from God because He knew that God labored under perfect righteousness.

Thus, God was *required* to banish Adam and Eve as he had banished Satan. (Genesis 3:1 and Genesis 3:23) But God, knowing what Satan would do, had already provided a way for Adam and Eve, and the generations to follow, to escape the captivity of Satan through the sacrifice which Christ would bring. The forgiveness of sin would break the captivity Satan exercised over man and allow man to return to God. Thus Christ offered Himself as the perfect sacrifice by which the sins of man could be forgiven. (John 1:29) At every turn, Satan interfered with God's plan, trying to destroy those who tried to follow God, because when God collected the number of souls He desired for His new creation, Satan would be bound forever. Thus Satan is fighting for his freedom when trying to draw us into sin. In His quest that every man be afforded the same opportunity to return to Him, God also provided for those who died in sin both *before* and after Christ brought His sacrifice. He did this by creating a means of testimony in eternity while grace is still available on earth. To fulfill this promise, Christ entered hell after His death to give testimony of His triumph to those who had died in their sins before He could bring His perfect sacrifice. (Luke 24:46) He told them that now they too could find forgiveness. (1Timothy 2:4) Then Christ went to His Apostles and commissioned them to teach God's children of His sacrifice for them, and to also teach them to pray for those who died in sin. A specific amount of time has been allotted in God's Plan of Salvation for His chosen ones to be made ready. (Acts 1:6-7) When that time is up, God will send His Son back to earth for the First Resurrection (Revelation 20:5) when He will take to heaven both those from eternity who have obtained forgiveness and those alive who have remained faithful. (11 Peter 3:10) When they are gone, grace will also be gone, and the final destruction of the end times will begin on the earth where, among other things, **one-third of all the people on earth will die.** When the destruction ends, God will send His Son back to earth with those He had taken at the First Resurrection who had been given celestial (perfect) bodies. They will reign with Christ as kings and priests for one thousand years and bring testimony to everyone living or dead who was not taken in the First Resurrection. Satan will be bound during this time, unable to influence mankind, so all will learn about and accept God. But, after the one thousand years of peace, Satan will be loosed again for a little while so those who have now newly accepted God can be tested. (Revelation 20:7) Satan will wreak havoc on those not firm in their faith and many will fall and follow Satan again. (Revelation 20:2) Then the Day of Judgment will arrive when everyone will be judged, *except* those taken by Christ in the First Resurrection. Those who accept Christ and remain faithful after Satan is loosed again, scripture calls the "lambs", and they will be allowed to occupy the new heaven God is creating. But those who did not accept Christ or fell to Satan again when he was loosed, scripture calls the "goats", and will be cast into hell with Satan and tormented day and night forever. (Revelation 20:10 and 15) Those taken in the First Resurrection will reign with Christ in the new kingdom and never have to be judged because their sins were forgiven, and entirely wiped away by God. Heaven rejoices in these who remained faithful to God from the beginning. These souls are the specific number of souls which scripture refers to as the firstfruits and as the Bride of Christ. These souls are also mentioned in the Apocrypha. 11 Esdras 2:40-41 says, *"Receive they number O Sion, and embrace those of thine that are clothed in white which have fulfilled the law of the Lord.* ***The number of thy children whom thou longest for, is fulfilled:*** *beseech the Lord that thy people, which have been called from the beginning, may be hallowed."* Jude 1:6 tells us: *"And **the angels which kept not their first estate, but left their own habitation, he hath reserved in everlasting chains** under darkness unto the judgment of the great day,"*

"He that overcometh shall inherit all things; and I will be his God, and he shall be my son."
Revelation 21:7

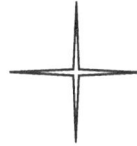

Chapter Nine

ARCHANGELS

Archangels are mentioned often throughout scripture. They bring God's messages to the people during critical times and appear to have the power to fight against evil. Michael, Gabriel and Raphael are the most familiar names bearing the rank of Archangel and the only ones mentioned by name in the canonical scriptures. **Michael** is most well known by his battle with Satan, when he threw him to earth and banished him from heaven after Satan waged war against God. Michael is therefore known as the angel of judgment. He is mentioned by name five times in scripture. In Daniel 10:13: *"...and behold Michael, one of the chief princes, came.."* and in Daniel 10:21: *"...but Michael your prince..."* and in Daniel 12:1 *"At that time shall Michael rise up, the great prince...."* Jude 9 tells us: *"Yet Michael the archangel...."* And in Revelation 12:7 we read: *"Michael and his angels fought...."* Michael is thought by some scholars to be the highest ranking angel thus a class of the Seraphim and is also thought to be the leader of the celestial armies. However he is also seen as the head of other ranks of angels within the angel hierarchy. Michael is also thought by some scholars to be the angel who will weigh the souls on judgment day. **Gabriel,** who is also mentioned in scripture, is best known for announcing that Mary was to be the mother of Christ. Luke 1:26-33 tells us: *"And in the sixth month the angel Gabriel was sent from God unto .a city in Galilee named Nazareth.........And behold thou shall conceive in they womb, and bring forth a son, and shalt call his* *name JESUS ...."* Gabriel, in Christian tradition, is known as the angel of mercy and associated with might, power, and strength. He is also known as the angel who prophesied to Daniel, the angel who strengthened Christ prior to the crucifixion, and the angel who struck down the cities of Sodom and Gomorrah. **Raphael** is considered in some literary references, to be the archangel of healing. He is often mentioned in the Apocrypha in the book of Tobit. *"I am Raphael , one of the seven holy angels. Which present the prayers of the saints, and which go in and go out before the glory of the Holy One."* (Tobit 12:15) This verse seems to indicate that there may be seven archangels and that these angels (and possibly others) move in and out of God's presence. Some scholars believe that Uriel, Raguel, Sariel and the fallen Lucifer are the names of the remaining angels in this rank although the names Metatron, Remiel, and Anael are also found in some references. 1 Thessalonians 4:16 says: *"For the Lord himself* *shall descend from heaven with a shout, with the voice of the archangel, and with the trump of God; and the dead in Christ shall rise first.*" Revelation 20:1-2 tells us, "*And I saw an angel come down from heaven, having a key to the bottomless pit and a great chain in his hand. And he laid hold on the dragon, that old serpent, which is the Devil, and Satan, and bound him a thousand years. And cast him into the bottomless pit, and shut him up, and set a seal on him, that he should deceive the nations no more.....*" Scripture tells us that God refers to us as His children, and wants us to mature in faith so that we can develop into the Bride of Christ. Romans 12:2 tells us: "*Be not conformed to this world; but be ye transformed by the renewing of your mind, that ye may prove what is that is good and acceptable and perfect will of God.*" We are also warned that because of the fallen angels and the power and bondage they exert over mankind, we must always be on the guard against them. Galatians 5:1 warns, "*Be ye not entangled again with the yoke of bondage."* We also learn from scripture that false prophets will come and we must be careful not to fall prey to their teachings because they are inspired by the fallen angels to harm the true faith. We are warned that while on earth we will *always* be surrounded with evil and that evil circles and tempts us every day through the fallen angels directed by Satan. We are told to remember their end, so that we will work to resist that temptation. A sacrament, or covenant with God contains certain rules for receiving the gifts we are offered to help us resist these fallen angels. **Holy Baptism, Holy Communion, and Holy Sealing are the three sacraments which have the power to re-institute mans' access to God.** They are prerequisites to being invited into the new kingdom which God is establishing for those who love Him. Scripture explains how the sin of Adam and Eve destined man to experience evil and denied them, and the generations to follow, access to God. The sacraments, however, allow us to access God once again and obtain God's protection, avoid the traps laid by Satan, and escape the consequences of our sins and the sins of our forefathers. We are clearly warned that if we are caught up in the harried pace of life and too busy to give God that which He asks, even believers may lose their soul salvation. Amazingly the Bible describes the conditions of the world when Christ returns and clearly predicts that many will be so engaged in their daily activities that they will be taken unaware and unprepared when the moment arrives. Matthew 25:40-42 tells us *"Then shall two be in the field; the one shall be taken, and the other left. Two women shall be grinding at the mill, the one shall be taken, and the other left. Watch therefore; for ye know not what hour your Lord doth come."* Sadly these verses and many others throughout scripture indicate that only *half* **of those who believe** they are ready for that day will be ready. Matthew 25:10-13 tells us: *"....they that were ready went in with him.....and the door was shut. Afterward came also the other*

WHAT DO ANGELS DO

virgins, saying, Lord, Lord, open to us. But he answered and said, Verily I say unto you, I know ye not. Watch therefore for you know neither the day nor the hour wherein the Son of man cometh." There are many parables and much instruction throughout scripture telling us that God has asked *all* men to make themselves ready for the return of Christ by learning of Him and striving to do as He asks. God desires that *all* men be saved and brings testimony to *everyone*. But as we read these parables and the words of the Apostles, we learn that though many are called, many will *not* accept God's invitation and will put forth a variety of reasons why they will not. Some are "too busy", some refuse knowledge about God, some fall into complacency and others bring harm to the children of God. Scripture warns us that no one knows when Christ will return. We therefore must always be ready. Matthew 24:36 tells us, *"But of that day and hour **knoweth no man**...but my Father only."* We also read that when those who spurn God's invitation realize that they are *not* a part of the First Resurrection, they will be in great agony. Matthew 22:13 says, *".... take him away, and cast him into outer darkness; **there shall be weeping and gnashing of teeth.**"* Scripture also tells us about the signs we will see as we approach the end times. Matthew 24:4-12,24 tells us, *"....wars, rumours of wars, famine, pestilences, earthquakes in diverse places, hatred toward Christians, betrayals, hatred, false prophets with signs and wonders, iniquity, no love"* Luke 21: 25 explains, *"And there shall be signs in the sun, and in the moon, and in the stars....the sea and the waves roaring....Men's hearts failing them for fear...."* And 2 Timothy 3:1-7 tells us, *"...in the last days perilous times shall come. For men shall be lovers of their own selves, covetous, boasters, proud, blasphemers, disobedient to parents, unthankful, unholy. Without natural affection, trucebreakers, false accusers, incontinent, fierce, despisers of those that are good. Traitors, heady, high minded, lovers of pleasures more than*

lovers of God; **Having a form of godliness but denying the power thereof....ever learning, and never able to come to the knowledge of the truth.** "
And, 2 Esdras 16:24 from the Apocrypha adds: *"At that time shall friends fight one against another..."*
We are also told about Christ's return to earth.   1 Thessalonians 4:16 tells us, *"For the Lord himself shall descend from heaven with a shout....then we....shall be caught up....to meet the Lord in the air....."*   1 Thessalonians 5:2 warns: *"For yourselves know perfectly that the day of the Lord so cometh as a thief in the night."*   2 Peter 3:10, 14 tells us, *"But the day of the Lord will come as a thief in the night.....Wherefore, beloved, seeing that ye look for such things, be diligent that ye may be found of him in peace, without spot, and blameless."*   Revelation 9:6 tells us, **"And in those days shall men seek death and shall not find it, and shall desire to die, and death shall flee from them."** Matthew 24:21, 22 warns, **"For then shall be great tribulation, such as was not since the**

beginning of the world to this time, no, nor ever shall be. *And except those days should be shortened, there should no flesh be saved: but for the elect's sake those days shall be shortened."* The "wedding feast" to which the bride of Christ will go will take place for three and one half years while the horrors of evil work upon the earth and all the satanic demons are unleashed. After this time elapses, Christ and those He took at the First Resurrection will return to earth to bring testimony to all who had once spurned His teachings. Satan and his cohorts will be bound during this testimony therefore everyone will accept God's offer. But then evil will be loosed again to test those who newly receive Christ's testimony. After this, *everything* **that is evil** will be bound *forever.* We are warned through scripture and also through a variety of venues by the messengers of God that if we are *not* prepared we cannot expect to be part of the First Resurrection. The parable of the five wise and five foolish virgins clearly demonstrates that for half of those who **proclaim** themselves a child of God, the door to salvation will *not* open to them. Matthew 25:1-13 tells this parable in its entirety, but the outcome can be found in Matthew 25:11, 12: *"......Lord, Lord, open up to us. But he answered and said, Verily I say unto you, 'I know you not."* There may be very little time before we are caught up in the terrors of the end times and little time to take note of our shortcomings, and make the necessary corrections. We are to prepare our soul as meticulously as a Bride prepares for her wedding. If we fail to do this and have not developed as God has requested, when Christ arrives for the First Resurrection, we will be rejected. But for those who *are* prepared, God tells us not to fear those days. He encourages us throughout scripture to be courageous. Psalm 27:14 tells us, *"Wait on the Lord: be of good courage...."* Psalm 31:24 says, *"Be of good courage, and he shall strengthen your heart...."* Isaiah 12:2 tells us, *"Behold, God is my salvation; I will trust and not* *be afraid....*" 11 Chronicles 19:11 states, "*.....Deal courageously, and the Lord shall be with the good.*" Nevertheless, there will be times when we are terribly frightened and our tears will flow and we will suffer. But, because of what we have learned we will know why, and know that help is on its way. We can be comforted by God's words in Revelation 2:10: *"Fear none of those things which thou shalt suffer...."* And in Luke 12:32: *"Fear not, little flock; For it is your Father's good pleasure to give you the kingdom."* And in John 14:27: *".......Let not your heart be troubled, neither let it be afraid."* If we are faithful and strive to learn of God and follow His precepts, we will experience the wonderful promise God reveals in Revelation 21: 4: *"And God shall wipe away all tears from their eyes; and there shall be no more death, neither sorrow, nor crying, neither shall there be any more pain....."* Matthew 25:21 promises: *".....thou hast been faithful over a few things, I will make thee ruler over many..."*

> *"And no marvel, for Satan himself is transformed into an angel of light."*
> *2 Corinthians 11:14*

Chapter Ten

ANGELS

The single word "angel" denotes those angels who are one of the three ranks of angels who are the messengers of God and occupy the third sphere of heaven. They are the lowest order of the angels but the closest in proximity to those on earth. They are the most easily recognized of all the angels, are concerned with and involved in the daily affairs of mankind and can minister to mankind. The most well known are those called 'guardian angels" who many believe are assigned to individuals to teach, guide and protect them.   Psalm 90:11 tells us: *"For **he hath given his angels charge over thee**; to* *keep thee in all thy ways.*"   Matthew 18:10 tells us *"See that you despise not one of these little ones: for I say unto you, that **their angels in heaven** always see the face of my Father who is in heaven.*" This tells us that even little children have guardian angels and that these angels apparently report directly to God.   Hebrews 1:14 tells us: *Are they not all **ministering spirits**, sent to minister for them, who shall receive the inheritance of salvation?*" This verse teaches us that those in the rank of Angels are thought to be imbued with the power to minister unto us.   Matthew 4:11 explains that they even ministered to Christ after Satan tried to tempt Him.   Angels are also believed to place ideas and thoughts into our minds, but ***cannot* in any way interfere with our free will.**   There are hundreds of references in scripture to Angels.   Many verses indicate that they can make themselves visible to us if they so choose to do so (Luke 1:11), that they can appear to look like man (Genesis 32:24), that they can appear as an Angel (Numbers 22:31), that they can talk (1 Kings 13:18), and walk, and that they answer questions (Zechariah 1:12). Angels are sent by God to perform a myriad of duties for God, and for and to mankind. In 1 Chronicles 21:15 we are told: *"And God **sent an angel** unto Jerusalem....."* And 11 Chronicles 32:21 tells us: *"And the Lord **sent an angel**, which cut off....."* Daniel 3:28 tells us: *"....who had **sent his angels** and delivered...."* Daniel 6:22 says: *"...God hath sent...."* And Acts 12:11 tells us: *"....sent his angel..."* Scripture also teaches us that we must be careful to show hospitality to strangers because we may be entertaining Angels unawares. (Hebrews 13:2) Psalm 34:7 tells us: *"The angel of the Lord encampeth round about them that fear him, and delivereth them."* Zechariah 1:10 says: *"And the man who stood among the myrtle trees answered and said, 'These are they whom the Lord hath sent to walk to and fro through the earth.".* What we learn from these words in scripture is that our Heavenly Father watches over us, is aware of our needs, hears our prayers, and has therefore provided the Angels for our education and protection. As our faith grows, so does our assurance that there is nothing which can occur in our life that God has not allowed and will use for our edification. As we learn to trust this truth, we develop the ability to endure our hardships with nobility. Because we know that from those experiences, God is developing our souls into those who will become the Bride of Christ, we welcome the opportunity to prove our loyalty, and to be tested and not found lacking. As we study the word of God we begin to understand that we *must* experience evil so we can appreciate righteousness. This allows us to *voluntarily* exercise our free will to choose between good and evil and that this is a choice which will have to be made by *everyone* at some point in time. We learn that there will be *no* evil in God's new kingdom, thus without our free-will consent, and our desire to spurn all things evil we *cannot be a part of that kingdom.* The Angels are given to protect the children of God when evil strikes and to help us endure those experiences. Psalm 18: 17-19 tells us: *"He delivered me from my strong enemy, and from them which hated me; for they were too strong for me. They prevented me in the day of my calamity; but the Lord was my stay. He brought me forth also into a large place; he delivered me, because he delighted in me."* This verse tells us that despite the hatred which Satan has for the children of God and the actions of those he sends against us, God protects us and brings us out of those circumstances which these demons of Satan can bring us. Scripture also teaches us that love can thwart the effects of evil. God loves His children with an everlasting and perfect love and wants us to learn how to love **in the same manner.** The love we know as humans can be fickle and shallow while the love of God is perfect and enduring. Matthew 22:37-39 says, *"Jesus said unto him, Thou shalt love the Lord thy God with **all thy heart, and with all thy soul, and with all thy mind.** This is the first* *and great commandment. And the second is like unto it, Thou shalt **love thy neighbor as thyself**."* Therefore we are to not only love God and the Lord Jesus, but also **love those whom They love.** Scripture also teaches us to watch, to test the spirits, and to be careful to stay under the protection of God. 2 Corinthians 11:14 warns: *"And no marvel; for Satan himself is transformed into an angel of light."*

There is a reason why God provides us with information about our future. He understands that as the end time prophesies are fulfilled, **the children of God will be persecuted and evil will prosper,** thus He wants us to be assured that He will care for us during these times as well. By understanding God's plan of salvation and what He offers, and knowing that our suffering is for a limited time, we can more easily withstand the days of evil and the wiles of Satan and his fallen angels. God also wants us to understand death and the torment that death and the second death will bring to sinners as opposed to the hope and joy offered to those who strive to be God's children. Those who remain faithful to God and have their sins forgiven will receive rewards which are so great that they are beyond description.

Throughout scripture God provides us with a glimpse of the new heaven and earth to strengthen us and to teach us the incredible wonder of what He wants to give us. As previously mentioned, one small example of this can be found when we read in scripture that the Apostle John, while on the island of Patmos, wrote about the streets of heaven being paved in gold. This was an analogy to help us comprehend the immense beauty of the City of God which those who remain faithful will enjoy. God calls the people who will be given these gifts His firstfruits. While others may enter heaven, this group will live and reign at God's side as the Bride of Christ. They are referred to as the overcomers, the kings and priests of His new world. Additionally, God provides for His children through scripture a description of what happens to them after death. Scripture explains that when Christ returns we will be given a celestial body which will never know sickness, sorrow, or death. 1 Corinthians 15:22 tells us: *"For as **in Adam all die**, even so **in Christ shall all be made alive**.* 1 Corinthians 15:35 says, *"But some man will say, How are the dead raised up? and with what body do they come? Behold, I shew you a mystery;* and 1 Corinthians 15:51 tells us, *"We shall not all sleep, but **we shall all be changed**."* These verses tell us that all men must die to their Adam-like nature, but that those who follow Christ will be made alive and will be changed. When the children of God rise again after death (or are taken at the First Resurrection) they will be transformed from a terrestrial or natural body to a celestial or spiritual body. 1 Corinthians 15:40 tells us, *"There are also celestial bodies, and bodies terrestrial: but the* *glory of the celestial is one, and the glory of the terrestrial is another."* And 1 Corinthians 15:44 says, *"It is sown a natural body; it is raised a spiritual body. There is a natural body, and there is a spiritual body."* 1 Corinthians 15:47-49 tells us, *"The first man is of the earth, earthy; the second man is the Lord from heaven....And as we have borne the image of the earthy, we shall also bear the image of the heavenly."*

These are incredible promises and revelations, but they also issue a warning which tells us that we must **labor** for this gift by being faithful, and by striving to learn of God and then do as God asks and **not bring harm to others**. 1 Corinthians 15:58 tells us, *"Therefore, my beloved brethren, be ye steadfast, unmoveable, always abounding in the work of the Lord, forasmuch as ye know that your labour is not in vain of the Lord."* Psalm 1:1-3 tells us, *"Blessed is the man that walketh not in the counsel of the ungodly, nor standeth in the way of* *sinners, nor sitteth in the seat of the scornful. But **his delight is in the law of the Lord;** and in his law doth he meditate day and night. And he shall be like a tree planted by the rivers of water, that bringeth forth his fruit in his season; his leaf also shall not wither, and whatsoever he doeth shall prosper."*

Here we learn who God will bless and thus what our behavior must be to be worthy of the celestial body which will rise at the First Resurrection. Although we all must die because of Adam, in Christ we will be made alive again. Psalms 1:1 tells us: *"walketh not in the counsel of the ungodly......but **delight in the law of the Lord."*** The children of God await the return of Christ who will take from the earth those who are worthy to become His Bride. They understand that God wants a bride for His Son who is filled with the desire and ability to love. Thus, God's children strive to overcome the self-serving Adam-like nature and develop a Christ-like nature to achieve this goal. They understand that a loving father who seeks a bride for his son would want that bride to be kind, longsuffering, and forgiving. They also know that scripture warns that only *half* of those who are *believers* will meet the criteria required to become the Bride. Therefore we must consider what will happen to those who, like the five foolish virgins, are left behind. These five foolish virgins were believers who thought they *were* prepared, but were not prepared for the arrival of the bridegroom, thus not allowed to go with Christ when He came for them. (Matthew 1:1-13, and 24:40-41) The Bride will be those whom God deems the "firstfruits", the "overcomers, and come from both the faithful still living on earth and the faithful from eternity and will love who God loves.

To be a part of the Bride of Christ is the hope of all the children of God but it **requires** the development of the Christ-like gentle nature of perfect love and goodness, and the spurning of *all* things evil. This then requires faith, and love, and the desire to be pleasing in the eyes of God. Although not all who believe will be found worthy to become the Bride of Christ, our Heavenly Father longs for all men to be saved. He has made provision that during the Thousand Years of Peace those not taken at the First Resurrection will have the opportunity to come to Christ and remain firm when Satan is loosed again. But when Satan is loosed *many* **will** lose their faith, and hatred and unbelief will gain in power once again and overcome many of these souls. Satan and his followers will have such great power, born out of anger and desperation that these new believers will be sorely tested and many will fall. When judgment day arrives, each will be openly judged and that judgment will weigh their faith and *all* **their past deeds**. *Every* deed will be **seen, weighed and judged** for all of mankind *except* those who were taken at the First Resurrection whose sins were no more remembered. Once all judgment has been issued, those who have done their best to remain faithful will become what scripture calls a lamb and can enter heaven, but cannot live in the City of God where only the *family* of God will reside. But if judgment day proves them *unworthy,* they will become what scripture calls a goat and experience the second death. The goats who allowed sin, envy, hatred and even complacency to govern their lives will be sent to the Lake of Fire for the second death where they will be in torment for all eternity. Thus, though not all are called to be the Bride, those souls who remain will either be a part of the kingdom of God, or will be cast into the Lake of Fire with Satan. **The second death is separation from God and from love *for all eternity* because the soul never dies.** There is *no* redemption from the second death, it is torment; it is evil for all eternity; *it is forever.*

These words may seem harsh but are a reminder that not all believers will be a part of the First Resurrection and become a part of the Bride of

Christ and thus the family of God. We need to clearly understand this truth so we strive to shed our old nature, become more like Christ, desire to leave all things evil, learn to love... and trust God and teach these truths to our children. God sees *everything* including the hidden recesses of our heart. He knows our motives and our faults and failings. However, God also knows our striving and hears our prayers to love more, to grow in compassion, to learn *and do* what He asks of us. The Bride of Christ will be expected to *desire* to be **perfect in her love toward others** by being, applying, developing, teaching, and giving love. When we truly love, we automatically desire to spurn what is not righteous in the eyes of God. We long to serve God and be with Him for all eternity where love will reign and evil will not exist. But if we spurn that which God offers and what is asked of us we may face the second death in the Lake of Fire which is a state of existence in a place without God, without righteousness, and devoid of love. It is the final and forever separation of good and evil. It is a place of torment, a place filled with anger, hate, jealousy, envy, intrigue, back-biting, slander, lies, plots, terror, and all things evil. It is a place to be avoided with every ounce of our being.

God wants us to be free of evil and to live with Him for all eternity in righteousness and love. He gives us every tool to do so and protects the path we must take to reach that goal. God's love for us is so great that He sent His Son to give His life so we could be saved from the captivity of the sin which Satan works to bring us. Sin dooms us to the Lake of Fire. God has given us the gift of scripture to help us learn. He has given us the angels who look after us. He wants all men to be saved and He wants us to succeed. He tells us in Jeremiah 31:3: *The Lord hath appeared of old unto me, saying Yea,* ***I have loved thee with an everlasting love:*** *therefore with lovingkindness have I drawn thee.* And He tells us in Revelation 22:17:

*"And the Spirit, and the bride say, Come and let him that heareth say, Come, and let him that is athirst come. And **whosoever will, let him take the water of life freely.**"* He has given the angels in heaven the power to bring us the messages God wants us to hear and to teach us, protect us and guide our path.

It does not matter what sins we have committed in the past if we now decide to learn of God and follow His precepts. God forgives us and gladly teaches us. **He teaches us how to take Holy Communion *worthily.*** Under His love and guidance we can grow to become those He longs to have with Him forever. The words in Romans 16:20 brings us comfort through the promise: *"And **the God of peace shall bruise Satan under your feet** shortly."* Therefore, we should say as Joshua 24:15 says: *"...As for me and my house, we will serve the Lord".* And while we wait we must... as John 16:33 and Acts 27:25 tell us: *"Be of good cheer".*

Bibliography

The Holy Bible, King James Version, published by The New Apostolic Church, Canada, Thomas Nelson, Inc., Camden, NJ, 1972

James Strong, LLD, STD, *Strong's Exhaustive Concordance of the Bible*, Abington, Nashville, thirty fourth printing 1996, copyright 1890

Ray C. Stedman, *Spiritual Warfare*, Word Books, Publisher, Waco, Texas, 1976

Sophy Burnham, *A Book of Angels*, Ballantine Books, New York 1990

Henry H. Halley, *Halley's Bible Handbook,* Zondervan Publishing House, Grand Rapids, Michigan, 24th edition, Copyright 1965

Henry M. Morris, *Many Infallible Proofs*, Moody Press, Chicago, 3rd printing 1977

Henry M. Morris, *The Bible and Modern Science*, Moody Press, Chicago, 1951, 1968

Donald Grey Barnhouse, *The Invisible War,* Zondervan Publishing House, Grand Rapids, Michigan, 12th printing 1976 copyright 1965

Robert Boyd, *Boyd's Bible Handbook*, Eugene, Oregon: Harvest House, 1983

About The Author

Helen Glowacki is an interior designer, writer, teacher, and motivational speaker. She was the host, writer, and producer of the television series "The Contemporary Woman", broadcast by UA Columbia Cablevision. Her writing credentials include an extensive background as a freelance feature and staff writer for four newspapers and for various newsletters and magazines. A graduate of William Paterson University, Helen received a Bachelor of Arts degree, magna cum laude, in Communications. She also received an Associate of Science degree with honors and is a registered nurse. She donates her books to cancer centers, drug rehabilitation centers, prisons, youth centers, hospitals, and also to the mission schools of *The Henwood Foundation* to use her gift for writing to help others find the love and comforting presence of God. She also emails books to those who are willing to receive testimony or will help in the quest to bring testimony to others. Helen writes amazing articles based in scripture which are filled with insight about how God wants us to conduct our lives and posts many on her Face book pages and on her website. Those who have provided reviews of Helen's books tout the beauty of the stories in her novels and many have noted that her non-fiction books are "spiritually uplifting and biblically correct". Her greatest joys are her husband, two children, four grandchildren, and time spent in her New Apostolic faith and in fellowship.

To order additional books, to become a distributor of these books, or for more information, visit the author's website at: www.helenglowacki.com or email the author at: helen@helenglowacki.com.

You can also visit her Face book page for her books at:
http://www.facebook.com/pages/The-Grandmother-
Series/155300907853909?ref=ts and also her personal page at:
http://www.facebook.com/pages/Helenglowacki/

Description of:
Do Our Little Sins Really Count?

Most of us are aware that murder and adultery and many other sins which bring harm to others, are displeasing to God, but few of us take the time to think about the less obvious sins we commit. Sins of commission, sins of omission, sin by proxy and the seven deadly sins are those thoughts and actions which we rarely consider. Yet scripture tells us that to be found worthy, *all* our sins must be wiped away. Scripture teaches us to seek Holy Communion and take it *worthily* so we can be forgiven our sins but that then we must *go and sin no more*. Thus we need to consciously *strive* not to sin. To do this we must look inward for those thoughts, actions and inactions which may not be pleasing to God and which scripture teaches us is considered sin. Without knowing God, knowing what He asks of us and why, it is impossible to please God. Therefore we strive to learn, strive to love, strive to overcome and strive to become what God seeks in the Bride of Christ. This sixth book in the *Why God Why* mini-series by Helen Glowacki provides her readers with another easy to read, easy to comprehend look at what God wants us to know and provides wonderful insight into how God works in our everyday lives.

ISBN 978-0-9847-2117-7

𝒩𝑜𝑣𝑒𝑙𝑠

by Helen Glowacki   (Book Size 6 x 9)

When God Broke Grandma's Heart: (208 pages) Rising from sorrow to become a beacon of faith Grandma struggles in an abusive marriage until God moves her from unequally yoked and broken to the healing of His love and forgiveness. Her granddaughter Sarah learns where to find answers to her problems and carries that legacy to those she loves. **Paperback: ISBN 978-0-9847-2110-8**

When God Took Grandma Home: (260 pages) About the heartache of drug addiction, of the enemy who destroys children through drugs, why God allows righteous anger, why we should pray for those in eternity and a description an incredible experience of faith for Matt and Sarah about why God allowed such heartache to occur. **Paperback: ISBN 978-0-49847-2111-5**

When Grandma Chased the Spirits: (208 Pages) The magnetism of idolatry, it's invisible power, and the heartache of bearing a child out of wedlock brings debilitating panic attacks to Mary and affects her husband Kevin. When Matt and Sarah tell them about their faith, God engineers a miracle to solve what that they thought impossible to resolve. **Paperback: ISBN 978-0-9847-2112-2**

The Granddaughter and the Monkey Swing: (284 pages) A wedding, a broken engagement, renovating and decorating a home through Divine Proportion, the truth about Halloween, and the gift of role models create a tender story of friendship. Helping through the planning and problems of a wedding culminates in the unveiling of a secret. **Paperback: ISBN 978-0- 9847-2113-9**

Grandma's Little Book of Poetry: The Story of God's Plan of Salvation: (277 pages) This beautiful whimsical story for all ages, begins when Sarah finds a manuscript in Grandma's desk and recognizes the story Grandma read to her and Josh and Caleb when they were children. Angels watch the inhabitants below them struggle to find God. **Paperback: ISBN 978-0-9847-2114-6**

Abiding Faith, Hidden Treasure: (262 pages) Serving in Iraq, Jim loses his faith to see a loving God allow so much heartache. Barbara invites him to dinner where Grandma shows him why creation and evolution co-exist and God's enemy creates the injustices Jim blames on God. Letters from the grave bring an incredible experience of faith. **Paperback: ISBN 978-0-9847-2115-3**

And Then They Asked God: (295 Pages) When Rebecca and Jayden arrive at their college campus they are overwhelmed by betrayal. Losing the values Rebecca once cherished fills her with guilt so monumental that she cannot forgive herself. Chaldeth the evil angel is defeated when God's grace frees Jayden and brings Rebecca's recovery. **Paperback: ISBN 978-0-9847-2116-7**

Caleb's Testimony: (262 pages) Caleb would have taken bets on his ability to trust God explicitly....until his accident.. Now, he and Ann must face the wrath of Satan aimed at causing them to blame God for their misfortune. Can they give up everything they worked for if God asks this of them? **Paperback: ISBN 978-0-9847-2119-1.**

The "Why God Why" mini-series

by Helen Glowacki (Book size: 5 ½ x 8 ½)

To What Purpose?: (126 pages) This first book in the *Why God Why* series answers questions about why we are here, what we need to learn, and what God plans for us. It is an excellent book for testimony and one you will share with others. **Paperback: ISBN 978-1-4507-7580-9**

Why God, Why?: (126 pages) This second book in the *Why God Why* Series describes why we experience heartache, its purpose, and how to face it. It answers questions about God's plan for us and what we need to do to be found worthy. **Paperback: ISBN 978-1-4507-7581-6**

Why Trust Scripture?: (126 pages) This third book in the *Why God, Why* Series addresses the challenges against scripture, who wrote the Bible, the importance of the sacraments, what role Satan plays, and how health and the Bible are related. **Paperback: ISBN 978-1-4507-7582-3**

What Should I Know about Life after Death and the Coming Tribulation?: (126 pages) What occurs following death, what will happen during the tribulation, and what the seven seals could mean to us are explained in this fourth book of the series. **Paperback: ISBN 978-1-4507-7583-0**

What Does God Want Me to do Right Now?: (126 pages) A concise explanation of what God asks of us, how we can live up to His expectations what is required to become a part of the Bride of Christ, and what God plans for the future with or without us. **Paperback: ISBN 978-1 4507-9076-5**

Do My Little Sins Really Count? (126 pages) Most of us believe that the little sins don't really matter but scripture explains why they do and teaches is about the seven deadly sins, sin by proxy, and sin by commission and omission which can affect whether or not we take Holy Communion worthily. **Paperback: ISBN: 978-0-9847-2117-7**

What Do Angels Do? (126 pages) Few of us know that there are three levels of heaven in which nine different ranks of angels exist. Nor do they know that these angels have been assigned three very different tasks. This little book takes the mystery out of what angel's do, who rules them, and how they affect our lives. **Paperback: ISBN: 978-0-9847-2119-1**

Non-Fiction Books

By Helen Glowacki   (Book Size 5 ½ x 8 ½)

Politically Incorrect: The Get Some Gumption Handbook For When Enough is Enough: (406 pages) Fifty timely and controversial issues are examined under the politically correct approach and compared to what scripture tells us is the approach that God wants His children to take. **Paperback: ISBN 978-1-4507-9074-1**

Overcoming Depression: How To Be Happy: (258 pages) We all face heartache, and all feel sad from time to time. But depression lingers and can result from many different causes. It can rob us of hope and destroy our relationship with God. Thus our Heavenly Father tells us through scripture how we can tap into His blessing and His direction and brings joy out of tribulation. **Paperback: ISBN 978-1-4507-9077-2**

What No One Tells You About Addictions: (216 pages) Discussing the merits of tough love, the selfish co-dependency of the enabler, what scripture tells us about spiritual warfare and invasion, and generational sin, make this book a must read. **Paperback: ISBN 978-1- 4507--9075-8**

Book Reviews

Reverend (District Apostle Ret.) Richard C. Freund, President of The New Apostolic Church, USA, Sea Cliff, New York: Magnificent writer, a story which makes the reader become emotionally involved, a joy to read, strong Christian values. *"When God Broke Grandma's Heart",* best seller quality.

Reverend (District Apostle Ret.) Richard C. Freund, President of The New Apostolic Church, USA. Helen's new novel, *"When God Took Grandma Home"* "Delights, brings comfort to those who grieve. Inspires, gives insight into the after-life, masterful portrayal.

Reverend Andrew Muliokela: New Apostolic Church in Alexandria, Virginia, formerly from Zambia Africa: *The Granddaughter and the Monkey Swing* and this series of books are awesome! A journey unlike another, I was reading a great novel, learning about confidence, love and support but also learning Bible verses at the same time! Helen Glowacki teaches through her books and I recommend them 100%. You'll enjoy the journey!

Reverend Frederick Rothe, (Ret. New Apostolic Church, New York) Palm Beach Gardens Congregation, Florida: Spent 48 years serving God and another 30 in the congregation. These books contain an accurate account of what God wants of us and why we suffer. The application of scripture and the people in the stories stand for the principles God wants in all of us.

Reverend Kevin Speranza, New Apostolic Church, Palm Beach Gardens, Florida: *And Then They Asked God* so happy I read this, weaves, documents biblical precepts, addresses political correctness, moral & political corruption, biased teaching, insidious growth of socialism renamed progressivism, self-importance, guilt and its debilitating power. WELL DONE! Identifies danger, artfully and Biblically addresses them.

Reverend Luke Jansen, Sr. V. P., Medical Connections, Boca Raton, Florida: "To Ms. Glowacki, author of **The Grandma Series**: grateful for your books, refreshing to find a Christian author who sees the *difference* between religion and spirituality AND that the two can and should be used in the same sentence.

Reverend Derryck Beukes, Montana-De Aar Congregation, Northern Cape, South Africa: Dear Helen, I personally often use your articles in my soul care visits, especially where youth are involved. I can assure you that your articles made a difference to my way of thinking, and I am busy encouraging fellow priests to read your works, as they are so factual and insightful! Thank you for your hard work. I thank God for you, and the wisdom He gave you! Please continue with the excellent work.

Deacon Shadreck Wilima, Overspill Congregation, Ndola, Zambia: Your articles prompt realistic examples which New Apostolic Christians need for their everyday living.

Youth Chairperson, Sunday School Teacher, Mulenga Ernest, Lusaka Central Congregation, Lusaka, Zambia: Through your writing I am constantly reminded of what to be aware of. I pray that God keeps you in the hollow of His hand, guards you and guides you to reach your brethren as you do me. Thanks for caring for the souls of many.

Reverend Aurelio Cerullo, Atripalda Congregation in Campania, Southern Italy: Dear Helen, your books and articles, and social networking bring brothers and sisters the words of our faith and touch the hearts of those who do not know our faith. Our goal isfound through the grace of the apostolate and in this sense, the word's from 1 Corinthians 15:58 assumes an important meaning: *"Therefore, my beloved brethren, be steadfast, immovable, always abounding in the work of the Lord, Knowing That your labor is not in vain in the Lord"*. Now that I am a minister of God for about a year I too am grateful to our beloved Father in Heaven for having opened the eyes of my soul, for having removed the plugs from my ears of my heart to hear and listen to His will in connection and communion with those who precede us, guided by the light of the Holy Spirit. God's work always evolves and adapts to the times and even via computers, cell phones and smart phones. I Thank God for having been able to know you, you're a very valuable pearl. God bless you richly.

Rev. Fred Krueger, (Ret.) Lutheran Minister 12 yrs and Clinical Social Worker 26 years, Dallas, Texas: "Inspiring, grabs the heart, author headed to the bestseller list, a pleasure to read, masterful. *"When God Took Grandma Home"* filled with insight into God's plan!

NOTE: The articles which are referred to in these reviews are excerpts from Helen Glowacki's non-fiction books. Not shown are reviews by the ministers who oversee *The Henwood Foundation*'s New Apostolic Mission Schools in Zambia and review all reading materials prior to distribution.

Edith Stier, wife of a Ret. District Evangelist, Clifton, New Jersey: *The Grandma Series* helps those in need, inspirational, heartwarming, ends with a beautiful example of how God explains our pain, renews hope, shows us the way, creates miracles. I love this series.

Patricia Robinson, wife of a Ret. Rector, Indiana: 5 star rating: *When God Broke Grandma's Heart*: WONDERFUL INSPIRATIONAL NOVEL, enjoyed this book, well written, Bible references, how to achieve peace of mind and soul.

Rosemarie Schaal, wife of an Ret. Reverend, New York: *Abiding Faith, Hidden Treasure:* Reader develops empathy, feels emotion, hears a battle between scientific and spiritual knowledge. Skillful, detailed, brilliant, vivid, teaches that nothing happens that is not planned by Him.

Colette van Loggerenberg, wife of a Minister, Scottsville Congregation of Pietermaritzberg, South Africa: *Grandma's Little Book of Poetry: The Story of God's Plan of Salvation:* This has to be one of the BEST EVER books that I have read....If you ever get the chance to get one of Helen's novels...READ IT. It's like a fairytale but a TRUE fairytale.....Close your eyes and picture this: Grandma with her hair in a bun, glasses perched delicately on her nose, sitting in a rocking chair and her grandchildren sitting on the floor with BIG eyes hanging onto her every word.....but with a twist!!!!! If you have doubts about PRAYER...read this book. I LOVED IT...thank you!

Debbie Espeland, wife of a Rector, Palm Beach Gardens Congregation, Florida: 5 star rating: *When God Took Grandma Home:* HEARTWARMING! This book touched my heart. It is both heartwarming and very spiritual.

Aletta Venter, wife of a Deacon, Scottsville Congregation, Pietermaritzburg, South Africa: *"Grandma's Little Book of Poetry: The Story of God's Plan of Salvation"*. What a learning process for me. Oooh I just **love** the way the angels are telling the story, **very original!** When is mankind ever going to learn? The inhabitant's lesson was to learn of good and evil. And they failed miserably each time. The devil has his agenda, and the inhabitants are the target. They call upon God for help, the angels rejoiced. Great....!!!

Aletta Venter, wife of a Deacon, Pietermaritzburg, South Africa: *"Abiding Faith, Hidden Treasure"* is the deepest and most rewarding novel I have ever read, touched my soul, made me cry, author's understanding of God's work is astounding, opens the mysteries

Lisa Mayo, wife of Minister, Palm Beach Gardens Congregation, Florida: Helen's *Why God Why* series of books gave me a new understanding of my faith. They are informative, so enlightening and in-depth, but in a way that is easily understood!!

Tammera Shelton, M.S. Psychology, Odenton, Maryland: I find *"When God Broke Grandma's Heart"* inspirational, beautifully portrays need to let go of negative events and that despite injustice, no pain is for naught.

Robert W. Rothe, USMC 1970-1976, Nevada: 5 star rating: *When God Broke Grandma's Heart:* Outstanding writer, kept me riveted, an angel sent to help through trying days. Thank you for helping me find peace.

Katharina Leipp, Schopfheim, Germany: This is the first time I have ever heard of a female New Apostolic author and I am very impressed by your articles. I have sent your link to my Shepherd and German friends and would like you to consider advertising in our German *Our Family Magazine.*

Claudine Visagie, South Africa: I'm trying to think of a way to introduce Helen's books and articles to others... especially to our youth. They are life changing!

Rabecca Mukuta Mukato, Lusaka, Zambia, Africa: Speaking on behalf of my Dad, District Elder Mukato, your articles are brilliant because they have changed me! Because of your articles my Dad has less headaches!

Robert Henry Parkes, Pietermaritzburg, South Africa: You are gifted with the verses and writings you do and are so inspiring to others. God is really using you as His special servant. You are really a wonderful person and we thank the Lord for you our sister in faith.

Frank Geores, from Port St. Lucie, Florida: *"When Grandma Chased The Spirits:* beautiful spiritual experience, can see caring nature and loving heart of author, eloquently reveals her love for God and search for truth. Worthy of the Star of Bethlehem rating. Thank you for sharing your magnificent gift.

Ben Lodwick, Avid Reader., from Brookfield, Wisconsin: Wow! An eye opener about God's plan of salvation, and why bad things happen to good people. Reminds me of Jim LaHaye and Jerry B. Jenkins "Left Behind Series". MUST READ!"

Dr. Walter Forman From North Palm Beach, Florida: *Grandma's Little Book of Poetry: The Story of God's Plan of Salvation:* a "wonderful book about success and failure in life. All Helen's novels are wonderful, a balm for the soul and an education to the seeker."

Susan Day, From Jupiter, Florida: *Abiding Faith, Hidden Treasure* : I hated to put it down, couldn't wait to pick it up, read all Helen's books, proves every point, shows what to do through God's words. I am 90 and Helen's books have helped me call on God.

Georgette Rothe, From Fort Piece, Florida: *Abiding Faith, Hidden Treasure* was more than I expected; a Biblical course making you re-evaluate your beliefs, enjoyed the journey very much.

Fred D'Alauro, from Palm Beach Shores, Florida: Internet 5 star rating: *When God Took_Grandma Home:* Remarkable! Inspirational, moving. Fascinating storyteller with a real message.

Debra Forman, Chester, New York. Internet 5 star rating: *When God Broke Grandma's Heart:* Written from the heart, shares the strong beliefs that shelters us in times of need, courage captivates the reader. Thank you.

Anonymous: Internet 5 star rating: *When God Broke Grandma's Heart:* WHEN LIFE GETS YOU DOWN, PICK THIS BOOK UP, it wrapped its arms around me. A wonderful read. Congratulations on an inspiring work.

A reviewer, a reader in Kentucky: Internet 5 star rating: *When God Broke Grandma's Heart:* Well written, heartwarming, overcoming heartbreak through God, touches your heart. A worthwhile read for all generations.

A reader: Internet 5 star rating: *When God Broke Grandma's Heart:* a must read for all generations. FANTASTIC!

A reviewer Internet 5 star rating: *When God Took Grandma Home:* Moves you, captivating.

A reviewer, a Kentucky reader: Internet 5 star rating: *When God Took Grandma Home:* MUST READ! Touching story of life's tragedies and how lessons learned from these heartbreaking events can turn into blessings.

Characters

in the novels by Helen Glowacki

Grandma: Grandma's life was filled with sibling betrayal and marital abuse. Her love of God, home remedies and famous boxing stance touches the heart.

Sarah: Sarah helps Grandma write her journal, learns about God's plan of salvation and the enemy who wants to harm her. She carries on Grandma's legacy of faith.

Matt: Matt, Sarah's husband, has a rock-like faith but when he loses a loved one, struggles with his anger with God, until he has a miraculous experience of faith.

Paul: Paul is Matt's older brother who earned a Captain's license for a seagoing tugboat. His faith sustains him despite enduring terrible circumstances.

Mary and Kevin: Mary and Kevin become Matt and Sarah's neighbors and friends. Mary's panic attacks end when God brings a miracle they never thought possible.

Elizabeth: Elizabeth adopts Rebecca, loses her husband twelve years later, is confronted with a potentially deadly illness and searches for Rebecca's birth mother.

Rebecca: Rebecca is Elizabeth daughter and Jayden's friend. Her father's death, the illness her mother faces, and a series of challenges at college almost destroy her.

John: John, a deacon, lost his wife to a debilitating disease, becomes Elizabeth's friend, and helps his daughter and grandson through a difficult divorce.

Jayden: Jayden is John's grandson and becomes Rebecca's friend. He has learned that prayer helps solve problems and he and Rebecca begin to share their faith.

Wade and Ruth: Wade is Jim's boss and friend who adopts two children from Iraq. Ruth is Jayden's mother and John's daughter who struggles to let go of the past.

Joshua and Debbie: Joshua, Sarah's younger brother, was demanding and judgmental until Caleb stepped in. Debbie looks to Joshua's family to be her role models.

Caleb and Ann: Caleb is Sarah and Josh's older brother and the family looks to him as they once looked to Grandma. Ann, Caleb's wife harbors a secret sadness.

Barbara and Jim: Barbara, Matt's sister is also Sarah's close friend. Her husband Jim plays devil's advocate in family debates, and matchmaker for his friend Wade.

Heza and Bara: Heza and Bara endured a suicide bomber attack when Bara was one and one half years old and Heza as she was born. They are adopted by Wade.

Chaldeth: Chaldeth is a fallen angel sent to destroy Grandma's family. He plots to bring great heartache to Rebecca and Jayden and their family to break their faith.

Durk: Durk, abused by a cruel father, is a sophomore at the college Rebecca and Jayden attend. He brings harm to Rebecca and Jayden but Jim gives him a second chance.

Professsor T. Nagorra, and Emils, and Dean Peerca:
These tenured professors befriend Durk and engage in activities which harm the students and the college campus.

Professors Doog and Sendnik, and President Legna:
These three share a faith in God, a love for their country, and desire to be role models. They help save the campus.

Richard and Rachel: Richard is a physician for whom Caleb built a house on the property next door to where he and Ann. live. Both couples share godly values and thus became friends.

Joe and Preacher: Both men work for the company which hired Caleb to supervise the construction of a shopping mall. Preacher is always trying to teach Joe what scripture says.

www.ingramcontent.com/pod-product-compliance
Lightning Source LLC
LaVergne TN
LVHW011207080426
835508LV00007B/647